A I
for Patches

Leigh Mackenzie & Noella Mackenzie

Illustrated by Patricia Hall

Dominie Press, Inc.

The development of the *Carousel Readers* was supported by the Reading Recovery project at California State University, San Bernardino. All authors' royalties from the sale of the *Carousel Readers* will be used to support various Reading Recovery projects.

Publisher: Raymond Yuen
Illustrator: Patricia Hall
Cover Designer:. Pamela Pettigrew-Norquist

Published by

Dominie Press, Inc.
1949 Kellogg Avenue
Carlsbad, California 92008 USA

ISBN 1-56270-366-8
Printed in Singapore by PH Productions Pte Ltd.

5 6 7 IP 99 98 97

On Saturday, Leigh wanted to give Patches a bath. Patches hates baths.

Leigh threw a ball to Patches. When Patches brought the ball back, Leigh grabbed him.

Into the tub went Patches.

Scrub, scrub, bubble, bubble.

Patches looked sad.

When Leigh was not looking,
Patches jumped out of the tub.
Down the hall ran Patches.
Leigh ran after him.

Bubbles everywhere!

"Woof, woof!" barked Patches.

"Come back, Patches," called Leigh.

"Now I've got you," said Leigh.
"Back to the tub you go."
Scrub, scrub, bubble, bubble.